ALICE GILBREATH

Fun with Weaving

ILLUSTRATED BY
JUDITH HOFFMAN CORWIN

William Morrow and Company   New York 1976

Printed in the United States of America.
1   2   3   4   5   80   79   78   77   76

Library of Congress Cataloging in Publication Data

Gilbreath, Alice Thompson.
  Fun with weaving.

  SUMMARY: Instructions for making some twenty gift or
household items using different weaving techniques.
    1. Hand weaving—Juvenile literature.   [1. Hand
weaving.   2. Weaving.   3. Handicraft]   I. Corwin,
Judith Hoffman.   II. Title.
TT848.G54   746.1'4   75-34006
ISBN 0-688-22063-0
ISBN 0-688-32063-5 lib. bdg.

BY THE AUTHOR

Candles for Beginners to Make
Making Costumes for Parties, Plays, and Holidays
Spouts, Lids, and Cans

CONTENTS

To my son, Rex, Jr., with much love.

INTRODUCTION

Weaving is an exciting art in which mind and fingers create together. It is simply the interlacing or intertwining of pliable materials, usually at right angles to each other. Some of the favorite materials are yarn, twine, thread, leather, vines, and stems of plants. A craft for all ages, weaving can be very simple or very complex.

Nobody is quite sure who first invented cloth weaving, but it is one of the most ancient of household arts. When the colonists arrived in America, many brought their spinning wheels and looms. The entire family helped to prepare and spin the fibers, and most of the cloth woven in the colonies was made at home. Some cloth weaving was done by journeyman weavers who traveled from house to house. Then some of the journeyman weavers stopped traveling and began weaving and selling their products. From this beginning, factories started and later weaving was done by machines.

Also among the ancient arts is basket weaving, practiced as early as 4000 B.C. Primitive people made clothing, ornaments, sleeping mats, cradles, and many household items from twigs, grasses, and roots.

Basketry is still a living art and should have a special interest for every American. The American Indians have developed basketry to a perfection never reached anywhere else. Today most baskets are factory made, but many are still woven by hand in countries where there is a large supply of natural materials.

There is something very special about handweaving, for it is always a one-of-a-kind item whether of clothing or basketry or decoration. There is also satisfaction in weaving a gift for a friend or something for yourself in which your skill and imagination has produced an object both useful and beautiful. Here are some suggestions for interesting projects that will also show you the basic techniques of weaving.

Directions given in this book are for right-handed people. If you are left-handed, you will need to reverse the procedures. All dimensions are given with width first and height or length second. The colors specified are only suggestions. Use colors or any combinations that are pleasing to you. Below is a glossary that explains the materials and special terms used in the text:

Basket-weaving Materials. Purchase #4 (thick) and #2 (thin) reed from hobby shops, or use natural materials such as vines with leaves removed. For spokes, use materials about ¼ inch in diameter, and for weavers, about ⅛ inch in diameter.

Cardboard. For looms, use heavy cardboard that will not bend easily such as from writing tablets or heavy cardboard boxes.

Glue. White household glues such as Elmer's Glue-All and LePage's White Glue are the most satisfactory. Apply directly from the bottle or with a tiny brush or toothpick.

Hardware Cloth. Purchase at lumber yards. It is sold

according to size of the squares. One-eighth-inch hardware cloth is called 8 x 8 mesh and has ⅛ inch squares. One-quarter-inch hardware cloth is called 4 x 4 mesh and has ¼ inch squares.

Lanyard. Purchase by the yard at variety stores or hobby shops. It is a plastic lacing about ⅛ inch wide and comes in many colors.

Loom. A framework used for weaving cloth or yarn materials. Looms used in this book are made of cardboard.

Sewing Stitches. *Buttonhole*—the thread is drawn up through the material close to the edge, cast over the edge, and drawn up again ½ inch from the edge. The next stitch is passed through the loop over the edge of the material, and drawn up. The stitches continue in this way, sewn closely side by side. *Overcast*—the thread is drawn up through the material and cast over the edge in long, loose stitches about ¼ to ½ inch apart. *Running*—the thread is drawn through the material in a small even stitch about ¼ inch long, running in and out.

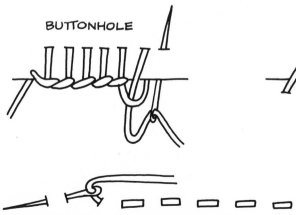

BUTTONHOLE

OVERCAST

RUNNING

Shuttle.   A holder for the weft as it is passed between the threads of the warp.

Spoke.   In basketry, spokes are heavy, flexible pieces of reed or other natural materials. They are used as the framework for the basket.

Warp.   Vertical threads or yarn. Usually the warp is threaded into the loom and interlaced with the weft.

Weaver.   In basketry, a weaver interlaces with the spokes by going in and out as it weaves around and around the basket. It is a long, flexible material, usually smaller in diameter than a spoke.

Weft.   Horizontal threads or yarn. They are interlaced with the warp.

SIMPLE WEAVING WITHOUT A LOOM

PARTY PLACE MAT

MATERIALS:

shelf liner (plastic or heavy paper),
   solid color, 16 inches by 12 inches
shelf liner (plastic or heavy paper),
   patterned, 11¼ inches by 14 inches
household glue

TOOLS:

ruler
pencil
scissors

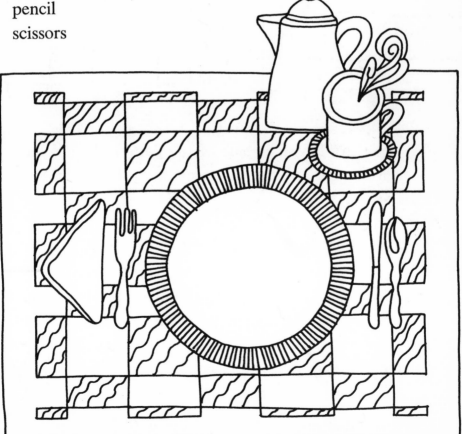

STEPS:

1. On the back of the solid-colored shelf liner, measure and draw an inch border all around.

2. Along the side borders, measure and mark distances of 1 inch, 2 inches, 1 inch, 2 inches, 1 inch, and 2 inches. Draw lines joining the measurements.

3. Cut along these lines (start the cut with the point of scissors). Do not cut into the border (Figure 1).

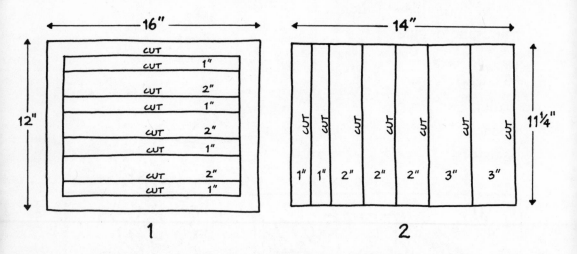

1

2

4. Along the 13½-inch side of the patterned shelf liner, measure and cut the following strips (Figure 2):
2 strips, 1 inch wide
3 strips, 2 inches wide
2 strips, 3 inches wide

5. Lay the place mat right side up on a flat surface with a short side nearest you. Beginning at the upper right corner, weave a 1-inch patterned strip horizontally across the place mat. Weave under the first solid-colored strip, over the second, under the third, and

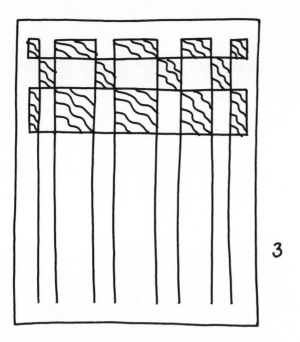

3

so on. Let each end of the patterned strip extend equal distances at the borders (Figure 3).

6. Weave a 2-inch patterned strip horizontally below the first patterned strip. Weave over where the first strip went under and under where the first strip went over. Be certain the edge of the second patterned strip touches the edge of the first patterned strip (Figure 3).

7. Weave a 3-inch strip the same way, weaving under where the second strip went over and over where the second strip went under (Figure 3).

8. Continue weaving in the same way, alternating the 2-inch and 3-inch strips, ending with the 1-inch strip.

9. Line up the ends of the patterned strips evenly, and glue the ones on top of the borders to the top of the place mat. Turn the place mat over, and glue the remaining lined-up ends to the back of the place mat.

PLANT HOLDER

MATERIALS:

2 white, plastic bleach bottles, ½ gallon size
black spray paint
red spray paint

TOOLS:

ruler
pencil
thin nail
scissors
cloth tape measure
white chalk

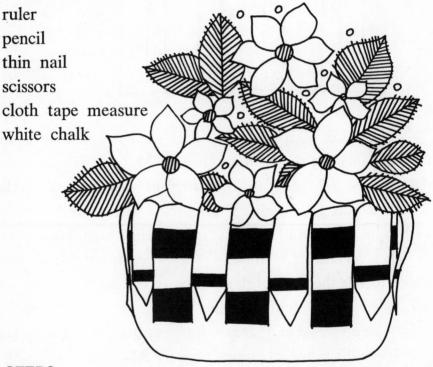

STEPS:

1. Remove labels from bleach bottles and wash them inside and out.
2. Fill the bottles with warm water. (This softens the plastic and makes it easier to cut.) Pour out the water. Ask an adult to help cut the bottles 5 inches from

the bottom. To start the cut, make a hole in each bottle with a nail. Discard the tops.

3. Paint the inside of one bottle red. Turn it upside down, and paint the outside black. Let the paint dry.

4. On the other bottle, measure and draw four rings: one ¾ inch wide, one ½ inch wide, and two ¼ inch wide. Warm the bottle as in Step 2. Make a hole in each line with a nail to start the cut. Cut out the rings.

5. Make twenty panels by cutting twenty slits about ¾ inch apart around the painted bottle. Cut each slit from the top down to an inch from the bottom. The panels will serve as the spokes of the holder. Taper the top ¾ inch of each spoke to a point (Figure 1).

6. Slip the ¾-inch-wide ring over the painted bottle on the outside of the spokes. Weave every other spoke over this ring. Push the ring down as far as it will go (Figure 2).

7. Slip one of the ¼-inch-wide rings over the bottle. Weave over this ring all the spokes that went under the first ring. Weave under this ring all the spokes that went over the first ring. Push the ring down near the first ring (Figure 2).

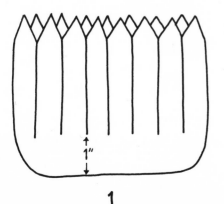

1

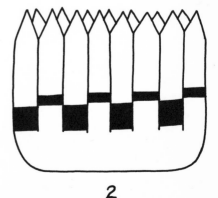

2

8. Slip the ½-inch-wide ring over the bottle. Weave it exactly as you did the bottom ring, and push it down near the second ring.

9. Slip the remaining ¼-inch-wide ring over the bottle. Weave it exactly as you did the second ring, and push it down near the third ring.

10. Take one of the spokes with the two ¼-inch-wide rings showing, bend it toward the outside, and insert it under the bottom ¼-inch-wide ring (Figure 3). Do the same with every spoke on which the two ¼-inch-wide rings show.

11. Bend all of the remaining spokes toward the inside, and insert them under the bottom ¼-inch-wide ring (Figure 4).

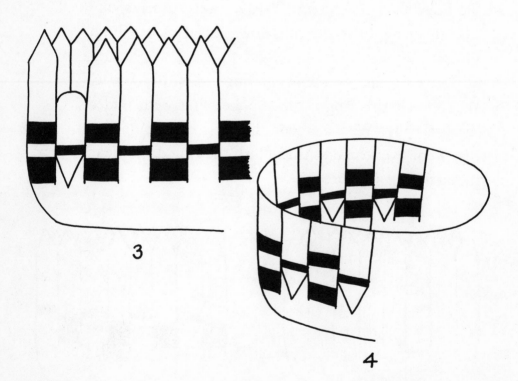

3

4

FISH MOBILE

MATERIALS:

cardboard box, ⅞ inch by 2⅞ inches by 2⅛ inches,
   such as 1½-ounce raisin box
cellophane tape
stiff ribbon, 2¼ yards, ¾-inch wide
household glue
aluminum foil
thread, 15 inches

TOOLS:

ruler
pencil
scissors
sewing needle

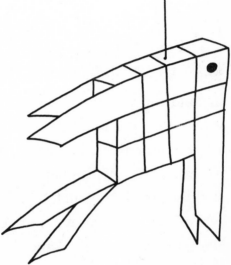

STEPS:

1. Close the top of the box and tape it shut. Stand it on a table horizontally.
2. Measure and cut ribbon into following lengths:
   1 strip, 22 inches
   2 strips, 10⅝ inches
   2 strips, 8 inches
   3 strips, 6½ inches
3. Wrap an 8-inch strip loosely around the lowest third of the box. Lap one end of the ribbon over the other

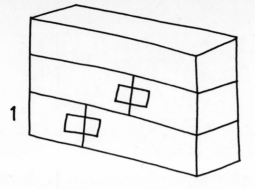

end and tape together. Wrap the other 8-inch strip of ribbon just above and touching the first strip. Fasten the same way (Figure 1).

4. Beginning at the bottom left corner of the box, weave a 6½-inch strip vertically around the width of the box. Weave under the first strip, over the second, around the top of the box, over the first strip on the other side, and under the second. Lap the end of the ribbon over the other end, and tape together.

5. Weave another 6½-inch strip vertically around the width of the box, touching the first strip. Weave over where the first strip went under and under where the first strip went over. Tape the ends together. Weave the remaining 6½-inch strip vertically around the width of the box, touching the second strip. Weave over where the second strip went under and under where the second strip went over. Tape the ends together (Figure 2).

6. Weave a 10⅝-inch strip around the box horizontally, so it touches the second horizontal strip. Weave over the first vertical strip on the right on each side of the box. Weave under the second vertical strip and over the third. Let the strip extend out on both sides. The

two ends will form a fin. Pull the ribbon gently so
the two ends of the fin are even (Figure 3).

7. Weave the other 10⅝-inch strip around the box vertically at right, so it touches the third vertical strip.
On both sides of the box, weave over the first horizontal strip, under the second, and over the third.
Let the strip extend out on both sides. The ends will
form another fin. Pull the ribbon gently so the two
ends of the fin are even (Figure 3).

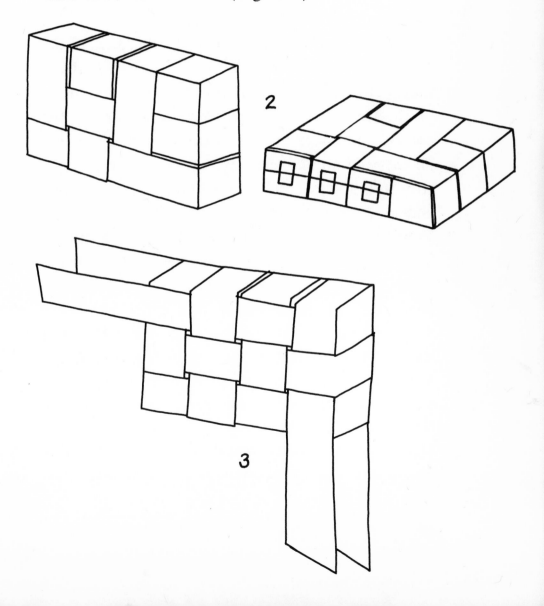

2

3

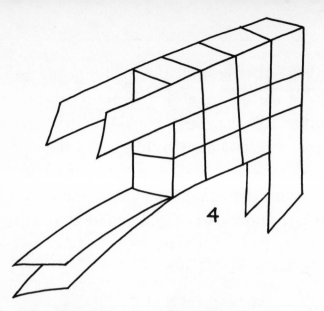

4

8. The 22-inch strip will go around the thickness of the box. Begin at the bottom left corner, weave horizontally, across the bottom, first under, then over, then under. Cover the bare space, continue around the corner, and under the next strip. Continue weaving all the way around the box. The unwoven ends of strip form the tail. Pull the ribbon gently so the two ends of the tail are even (Figure 4).

9. From the foil, cut two circles, each ¼ inch in diameter. They are the eyes. Glue one eye on each side at the corner diagonally opposite the tail. Cut off the ends of the fins and tail diagonally.

10. Thread a needle and tie a knot in one end of the thread. Pierce the needle through the sticky side of a ½-inch length of cellophane tape. Stick the tape, with the knot underneath, on top of the fish ¾ of an inch from the end opposite the eyes.

11. Hang the mobile where there is a slight movement of air.

STRIPED BOOKMARK

MATERIALS:

⅛-inch hardware cloth, 1⅜ inches by 5½ inches
black lanyard, 30 inches
yellow lanyard, 15 inches
blue lanyard, 37½ inches
household glue

TOOLS:

tin snips
scissors

STEPS:

1. Trim the rough ends off the hardware cloth with tin
   snips. Apply several coats of glue all around the edges,
   allowing each coat to dry before applying the next.
2. Cut all the lanyard into 7½-inch lengths.
3. Lay the hardware cloth horizontally on a table. Beginning at the upper right corner, weave a strand of black

lanyard through it. Weave under the first wire, over the second, under the third, and so on across the row. (Figure 1). Let the ends of the lanyard extend equally at each end of the hardware cloth.

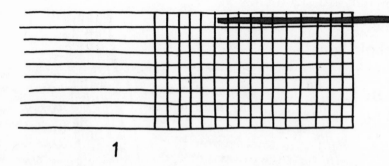

1

4. Weave another length of black lanyard through it in the row below. Weave exactly as you did the first row, weaving under the first wire, over the second, and on across the row.

5. Continue weaving in exactly the same way, using a length of yellow lanyard, then five rows of blue, another row of yellow, and two rows of black. Trim the fringes evenly with scissors.

WALL HANGING

MATERIALS:

paper, 8 inches by 10½ inches
⅛-inch hardware cloth, 8 inches by 10½ inches
household glue
4-ply yarn

TOOLS:

pencil
crayons
felt marker
tin snips
scissors
tapestry needle

STEPS:

1. On the sheet of paper, draw a large, simple picture such as a smiling face. With crayons, color the picture in two or three colors that please you. Color the rest of the sheet (the background) another color. If your picture is done in light colors, use a dark color for the background and vice versa. You may want to include touches of the background color in your picture.

2. Trim the rough ends off the hardware cloth with tin snips. Apply glue to the rough places. Let the glue dry.

3. Lay your picture on a table, and place the hardware cloth over it. With a felt marker, trace the lines of the picture on the hardware cloth.

4. Thread the tapestry needle with 1½ yards of yarn in the color you will be using the least. Pull the ends of the yarn even. Insert the needle from the underside of the hardware cloth up through one hole at an edge of this color area. Leave a 6-inch length underneath. Weave the double strand of yarn up and down through the holes in the hardware cloth wherever this color is used. When weaving a single curved line, stitch up and down diagonally over the wires to make the line curve, even though the stitch will not cover the entire square (Figure 1). Also use a diagonal stitch when the picture comes to a point. If you are weaving large areas in straight lines, when you reach the end of the picture in one direction, weave back in the other direction (Figure 2). In each place where this color in your picture ends, insert the needle through to the wrong side. Cut off the

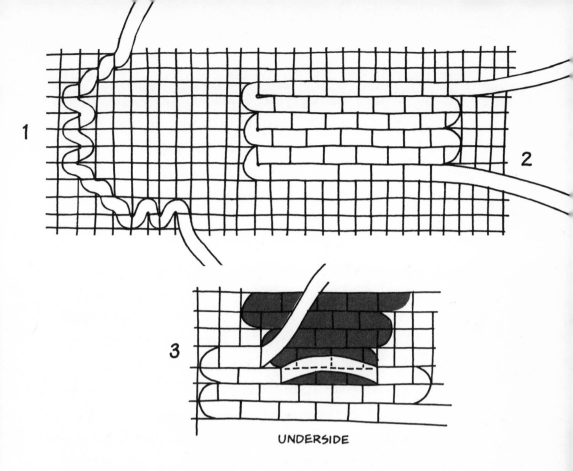

UNDERSIDE

yarn, leaving 6-inch ends. Start again where the same color appears, each time leaving 6-inch lengths of yarn underneath when you start and when you finish. Weave each of these hanging strands through the yarn an inch along the back, and cut off.

5. Weave each color, except the background color, in the same way. When you come to yarn of another color, skip across it on the underside and bring the yarn up in the next empty or partly empty square (Figure 3).

6. Weave the background color last. Thread a 24-inch length of the background color. Do not pull the strands even, since you will be weaving with a single strand.

Simple Weaving Without a Loom   23

Lay the wall hanging on the table with the lower part of the picture facing you. Start at the upper right corner, leaving a 6-inch strand underneath, and weave in and out horizontally across the top row of the hardware cloth. When you come to the edge of the hardware cloth, loop the yarn over it, then weave back horizontally to the other side. In the second row, weave over where the first row went under and under where the first row went over. When you come to the edge of another color of yarn, skip across the back of the picture and start again in the next open or partly open space. Be certain to weave each row over where the row before it went under and under where the row before it went over (See Figure 2). When the yarn becomes short, insert the needle through to the underside, weave an inch into the woven part, and cut off. Thread the needle and continue weaving. Weave all hanging strands an inch into the back of the woven part and cut off.

7. Beginning at the top right corner, loop yarn of the background color around the top of each square of the hardware cloth all the way across (Figure 4). Weave both ends into the back of the wall hanging. Repeat

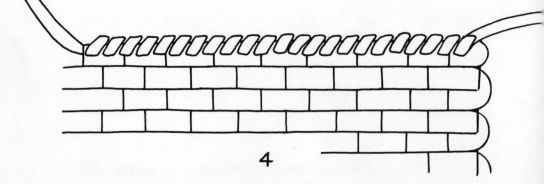

4

the same step at the bottom of the wall hanging, beginning at the bottom right corner.

8. Thread a needle with 30 inches of yarn in the background color. Knot the two ends together. In one of the corners at the back top of the picture, draw the yarn through a few stitches. Bring the needle to the other corner, and draw the yarn through several stitches there. Cut the yarn, remove the needle, and tie a knot (Figure 5). Hang your picture on a small, thin nail or a push pin.

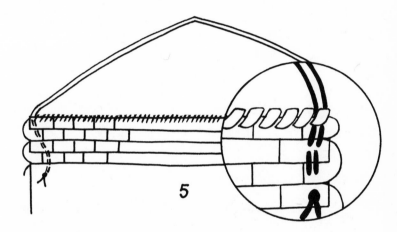

5

CLUTCH BAG

MATERIALS:

4-ply yarn, 55 yards
loosely woven dishcloth, 11½ inches by 13½ inches
cloth for lining, any color,
    11½ inches by 13½ inches
thin cardboard, 10½ inches by 12¾ inches
thread
bead or button

TOOLS:

scissors
ruler
tapestry needle
straight pins
clothespins
sewing needle

STEPS:

1. Thread a tapestry needle with 2 yards of yarn, and pull the ends even.

2. Lay the dishcloth vertically on a flat surface. At the upper right-hand corner, tie the two ends of the yarn together around the first double strand of threads of dishcloth. Weave under the second double strand of threads, over the third, and continue horizontally all the way across the first row.

3. If the last stitch of the first row was over, begin the next row by weaving under. If the last stitch of the first row was under, begin by weaving over. Weave back across the second row (Figure 1).

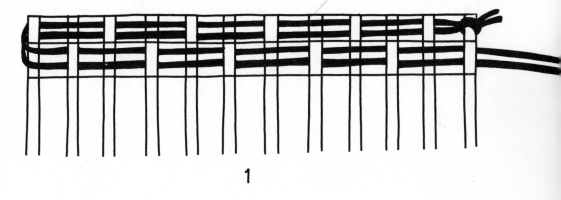

1

4. Continue weaving in the same way until the dishcloth is covered with yarn. When the yarn becomes short, clip the ends. Thread more yarn and tie the ends of the new yarn to the ends of the woven yarn. Continue weaving, being sure that all knots are tied on the underside of the dishcloth. When the dishcloth is completely woven, clip and tie the two pieces of yarn

together around the last double strand of threads in the corner of the dishcloth.

5. Lay the wrong side of the lining on the wrong side of the dishcloth. Pin ¼ inch of the lining under along both short sides. Sew the lining to the dishcloth with an overcast stitch ¼ inch from the edges (Figure 2).

6. Along one long side, sew the lining to the clutch bag ½ inch from the edge using a running stitch (Figure 3).

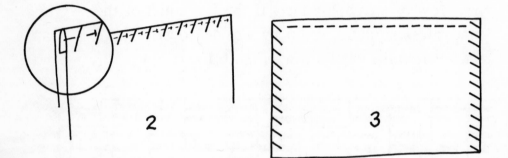

2   3

7. Slip the cardboard into the bag under the lining. Sew the lining to the bag ½ inch from the open edge using a running stitch.

8. Fold the bag double 4¾ inches down from one short side. Clip a few clothespins to the folded part to hold it in place while you sew.

9. Lay the bag on a flat surface with the fold nearest you. Thread the tapestry needle with about 30 inches of yarn. Beginning an inch above the lower left corner, weave the needle in and out to the end of the corner (Figure 4). Then, using a buttonhole stitch, about

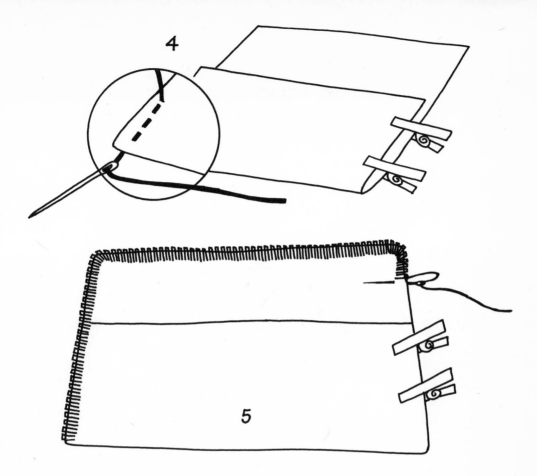

½ inch deep, sew up the side of the bag, across the top, and down the other side. When the yarn becomes short, weave in and out near the outer edge for about an inch and cut off. Thread more yarn. Weave in and out near the outer edge for about an inch, and continue the buttonhole stitching where you left off (Figure 5). Finish by weaving the yarn back in and out of the stitches for an inch. Cut off yarn.

10. Fold the top of the clutch bag down 3½ inches to form a flap. In the center of the bag ⅛ inch below the flap, sew a bead or button to the outer layer of the clutch bag with yarn. Tie securely, and cut off yarn. Make a loop in the center of the flap by drawing a needle, threaded with double yarn, up from the underside at the inner edge of the border, leaving 4 inches of yarn underneath. Insert the needle through to the under-

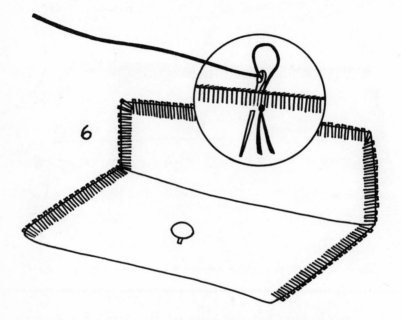

side (Figure 6). Adjust the yarn so the loop is large enough to fit snugly around the bead or button. Cut off the yarn, and tie the yarn ends together. Trim the ends.

SPOOL WEAVING

GOLDEN STRETCH NECKLACE

MATERIALS:

gold-colored elastic thread, 13 yards

TOOLS:

large wooden spool
1-inch wire nails, 4
small hammer
pencil
ruler
6-penny nail
   (2 inches long)
sewing needle
scissors

STEPS:

1. Drive the four wire nails ⅜ inch into the top of one end of the spool, equal distances apart (Figure 1).

2. Six inches from one end of the elastic thread, tie a loose knot around one nail and insert the short end of the thread down the center of the spool. Moving counterclockwise to the next nail, bring the thread across on the side facing the center of the spool, loop it around the nail, and then on to the next nail. Thread the two remaining nails the same way (Figure 2).

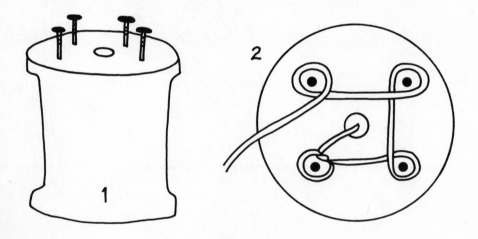

3. Bring the thread across the first nail, near its top, on the side facing away from the center of the spool. With the 6-penny nail, pick up the lower thread and lift it over the new thread and over the nail toward the center of the spool. Move the thread on to the top part of the next nail on the side facing away from the center of the spool. Repeat picking up the lower thread and lifting it over the new thread and the nail toward

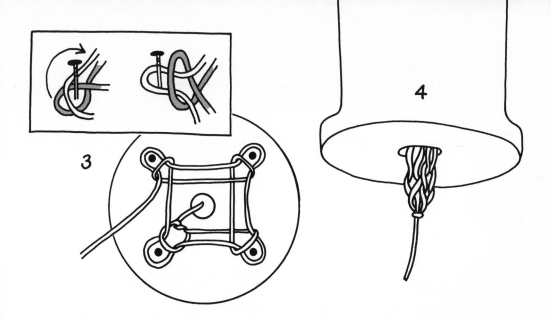

the center of the spool. Do the same thing at the next two nails (Figure 3).

4. Continue weaving around and around the spool. The elastic tube will come out of the hole at the bottom of the spool. Pull down gently on the tube after each circle of weaving (Figure 4).

5. Weave until you have 24 inches of tubing. Cut the thread off, leaving a 4-inch piece.

6. Carefully slip the loop off each nail. Insert the thread through each loop and pull tight (Figure 5).

7. Remove necklace from the spool. Tie the two ends of thread securely together. Cut off. Reinforce by sewing elastic thread through a few outside loops on each side and tying together. Cut off thread.

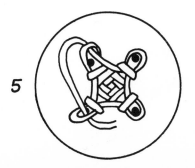

GROVER, THE GARDEN SNAKE

MATERIALS:

4-ply green yarn, 7½ yards
4-ply orange yarn, 6 inches
10-inch pipe cleaner

TOOLS:

large wooden spool
1-inch wire nails, 5
small hammer
pencil
ruler
6-penny nail
   (2 inches long)
scissors
plastic straw,
   8 inches long and
   ¼ inch in diameter
upholstery needle

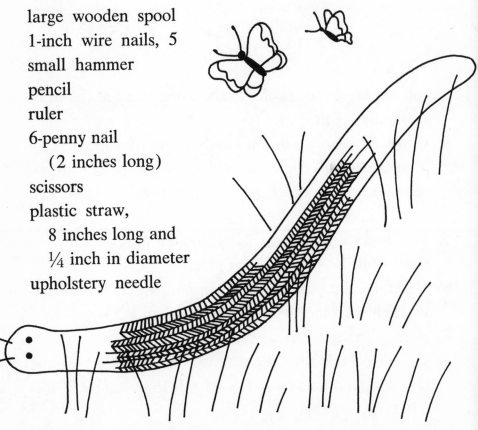

STEPS:

1. Drive the five wire nails ⅜ inch into the outer part of the spool equal distances apart (Figure 1).

2. Six inches from one end of the yarn, tie a loose knot around one nail and insert the short end of the yarn down the center of the spool. Moving counterclockwise to the next nail, bring the yarn across on the side facing the center of the spool, loop it around the nail, and then on to the next nail. Thread the three remaining nails the same way (Figure 2).

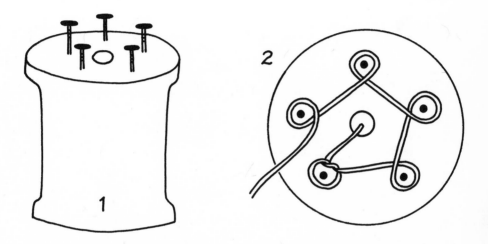

3. Bring the yarn across the first nail, near its top, on the side facing away from the center of the spool. With the 6-penny nail, pick up the lower yarn and lift it over the new yarn and over the nail toward the center of the spool. Move the yarn on to the top part of the next nail on the side facing away from the center of the spool. Repeat picking up the lower yarn and lifting it over the new yarn and over the nail toward the center of the spool. Do the same thing at the next three nails (Figure 3).

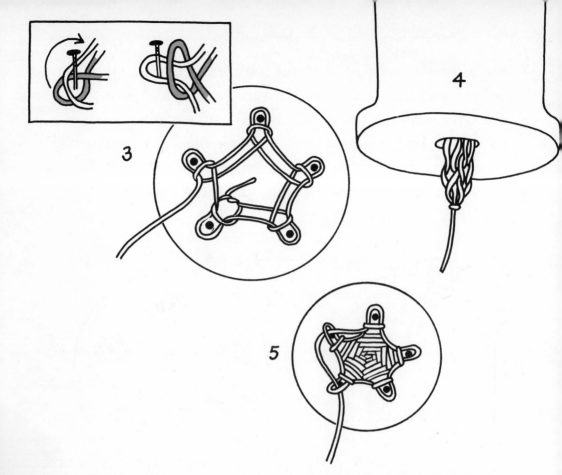

4. Continue weaving around and around the spool. The yarn tube will come out of the hole at the bottom of the spool. Pull down gently on the tube after each circle of weaving (Figure 4).

5. Weave until 4 inches of yarn remain. Carefully slip the loop off each nail. Insert the end of the yarn through each loop and pull tight (Figure 5). Remove the tube from the spool.

6. Insert the straw into the tube from the open end, leaving ½ inch outside the tube.

7. Bend back tightly ¼ inch of each end of the pipe cleaner. Insert the pipe cleaner into the straw. With thumb and index finger, hold the pipe cleaner at the closed end of the tube while you remove the straw.

8. Sew the open end of the tube together with the yarn remaining there. Tie a knot and cut off. It is Grover's head.

9. Insert a needle threaded with orange yarn into the center front of the head and up to the top of the head on one side, leaving a ½-inch piece extending. Sew a small stitch for an eye. Bring the needle up on the other side of the head, and sew another small stitch for the other eye. Bring the needle down alongside the yarn extending at front of head. Cut the yarn ends, leaving ¼ inch for fangs (Figure 6). Bend the body to look like a garden snake.

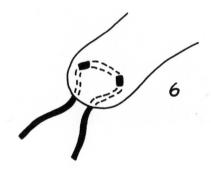

6

RUG

MATERIALS:

4-ply yarn, several colors, 220 yards

TOOLS:

large wooden spool

1-inch wire nails, 4

small hammer

pencil

ruler

6-penny nail
    (2 inches long)

scissors

upholstery needle

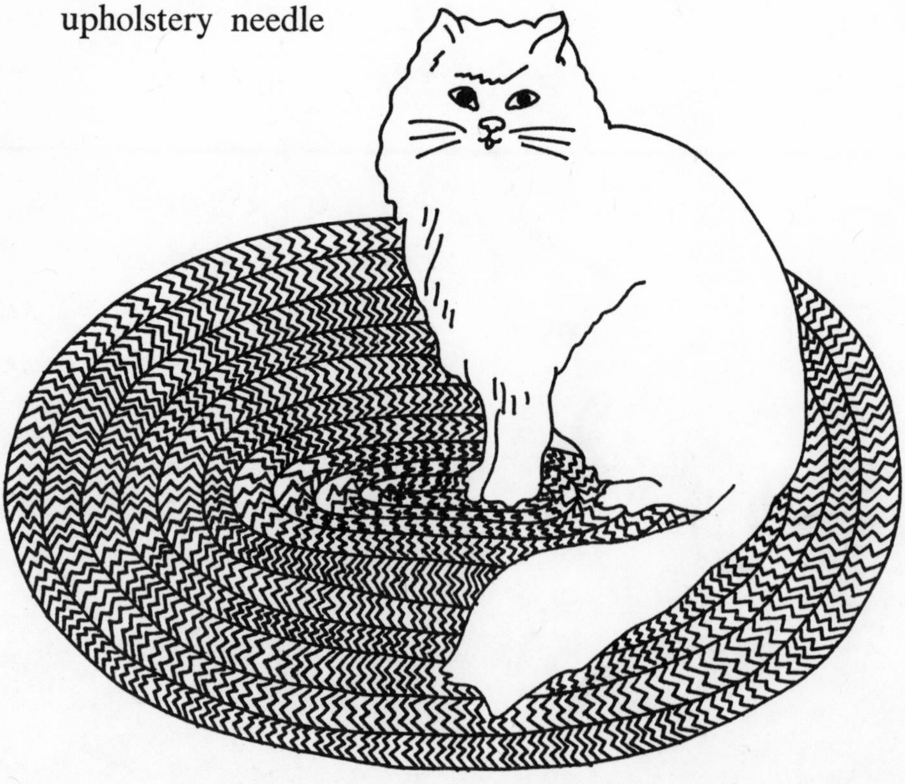

STEPS:

1. Drive the four wire nails ⅜ of an inch into the top of one end of the spool equal distances apart (Figure 1).

2. Six inches from one end of the yarn, tie a loose knot around one nail, and insert the short end of the yarn down the center of the spool. Moving counterclockwise to the next nail, bring the yarn across on the side facing the center of the spool, loop it around the nail, and then on to the next nail. Thread the two remaining nails the same way (Figure 2).

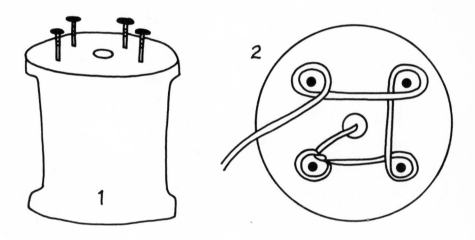

3. Bring the yarn across the first nail, near its top, on the side facing away from the center of the spool. With the 6-penny nail, pick up the lower yarn and lift it over the new yarn and the nail toward the center of the spool. Move the yarn on to the top part of the next nail on the side facing away from the center of the spool. Repeat picking up the lower yarn and lifting it over the new yarn and the nail toward the center of

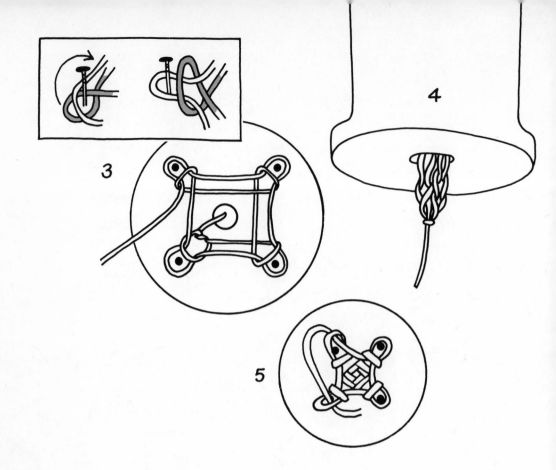

the spool. Do the same thing at the next two nails (Figure 3).

4. Continue weaving around and around the spool. When the yarn becomes very short, tie on a piece of another color, and continue weaving. The yarn tube will come out the hole at the bottom of the spool. Pull it down gently after each circle of weaving (Figure 4).

5. Continue until you have 12½ yards of yarn tubing. Cut the yarn off, leaving a 4-inch piece.

6. Carefully slip the loop off each nail. Insert the end of the yarn through each loop and pull tight (Figure 5). Remove the tube from the spool.

40 Spool Weaving

7. Lay 1½ inches of tubing in a straight vertical line on a flat surface. Bend in half at the bottom to the right to make a double row. Thread an upholstery needle with yarn, knot it at one end, and sew the two lengths of tubing together with an overcast stitch. Be sure the tubing lies flat while you sew. Make the stitches about ⅜ inch apart with each stitch reaching halfway across each length of tubing (Figure 6).

8. Loop the tubing around the top end counterclockwise, and sew in place in the same way. Continue looping the tubing counterclockwise, around and around, sewing it in place as you go (Figure 7). When the sewing yarn becomes short, tie a knot and cut off the ends of yarn. Thread the needle with more yarn, tie a knot, and continue sewing, keeping all knots on the underside. Tie the sewing yarn to the end of the yarn on the tube. Then sew the end of the tube to the rug with a few overcast stitches. Tie a knot, and cut off the ends of yarn.

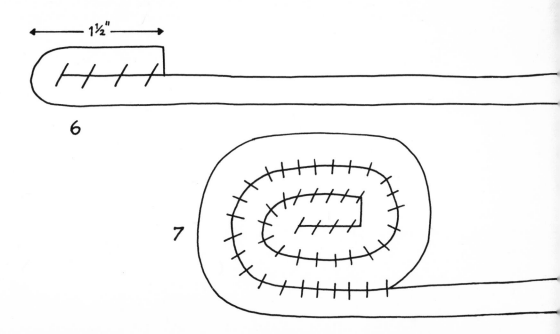

FINGER WEAVING

BELT

MATERIALS:

cotton rope,
   ¼ inch in diameter,
   4 yards

TOOLS:

ruler
heavy scissors

STEPS:

1. Tie a loose knot 15 inches from one end of the rope, leaving a loop large enough for your thumb to go through. Hold the knot in your left hand so that the

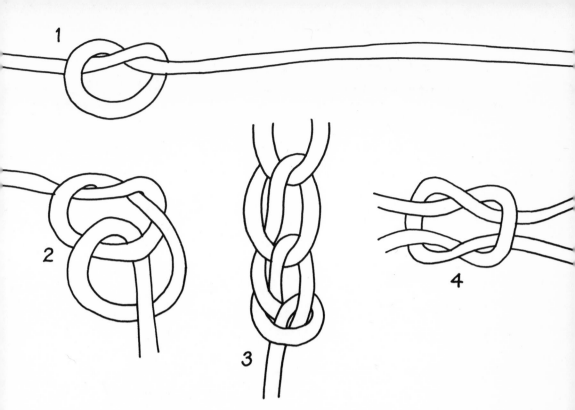

loop is at the bottom and the longer end of rope goes over the knot at the upper right side (Figure 1).

2. With your right hand, insert the longer length of rope up through the loop, and pull down to form another loop (Figure 2). This is finger weaving.

3. Insert the rope up through the second loop, and pull down to form another loop. Letting your left hand slide along one loop behind the right hand, continue weaving in the same way until the chain is long enough to reach around your waist.

4. Make the last loop as before, and pull tight (Figure 3).

5. Cut the rope off, leaving a 15-inch length. Tie a knot in each end of the belt to keep it from raveling.

6. Tie at the waist with a square knot (Figure 4).

CHRISTMAS GARLAND

MATERIALS:

rug yarn, red or green, 30 yards
heavy cord, gold or silver, 15 yards

TOOLS:

ruler
scissors

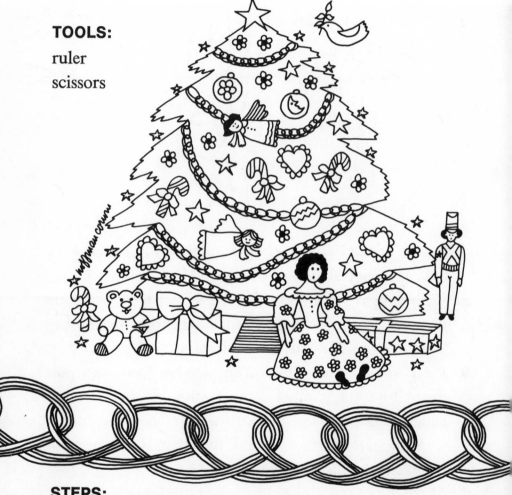

STEPS:

1. Cut the yarn into two equal lengths.
2. Hold the ends of the two lengths of yarn and the cord together in your left hand. Tie a knot ½ inch from the

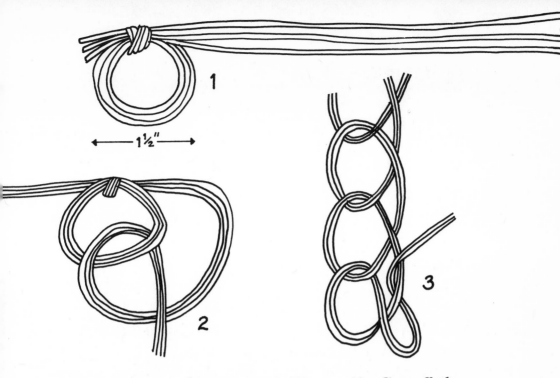

ends, leaving a 1½-inch loop (Figure 1). Cut off the short lengths of yarn and cord.

3. Hold the knot in your left hand with the loop hanging down and the lengths of yarn and cord behind it. With your right hand, insert the three strands up through the loop, and pull down to form another loop (Figure 2). This is finger weaving.

4. Insert the three strands up through the second loop, and pull down to form another loop. Continue in the same way until 6 inches of strands remain.

5. Insert the strands up through the last loop as before. Insert the ends of the yarn and cord through the space between the last two loops, and pull tight (Figure 3). Cut off ends.

6. Use on Christmas tree or for other Christmas decoration.

CURTAINS

A GOOD GROUP PROJECT

MATERIALS:

twine or cord
beads

TOOLS:

ruler or yardstick
scissors

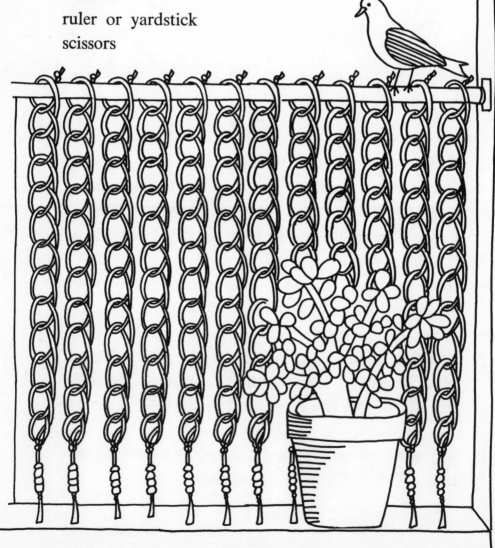

STEPS:

1. Measure the height of the window you are making the curtain for. Each length of twine should be four times the height of the window. Each woven length of twine will cover about 1½ inches of the width of the window. Measure to get the number of lengths of twine you will need. Cut twine into proper lengths.

2. Double the end of one length back 3 inches. Tie the double strand in a knot, leaving a 1¼-inch loop (Figure 1).

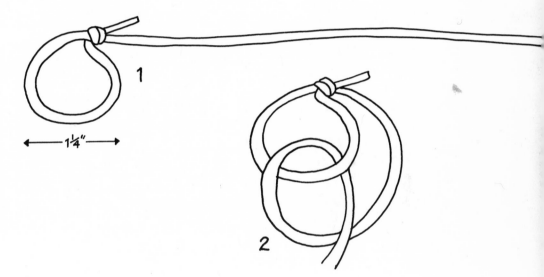

3. Hold the knot in your left hand with the loop hanging down and the twine behind it. With your right hand, insert the twine up through the loop, and pull down to form another loop (Figure 2).

4. Insert the twine up through the second loop, and pull down to form another loop. Continue in the same way until 4 inches of the twine remain.

5. Insert the twine up through the last loop as before. Insert the end of the twine through the space between the last two loops, and pull tight (Figure 3).
6. Thread several beads on the end of each chain, and tie a knot. The beads will act as a weight to make the chain hang straight (Figure 4).
7. Hang the chains on the curtain rod by the top loops.

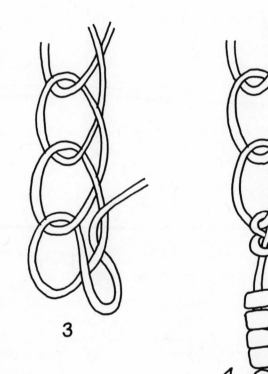

3

4

PENDANT

MATERIALS:

¼-inch hardware cloth,
  1½ inches by 1½ inches
household glue
black spray paint
red lanyard, 4 yards
black lanyard, 1 yard 8 inches

TOOLS:

tin snips
ruler
scissors

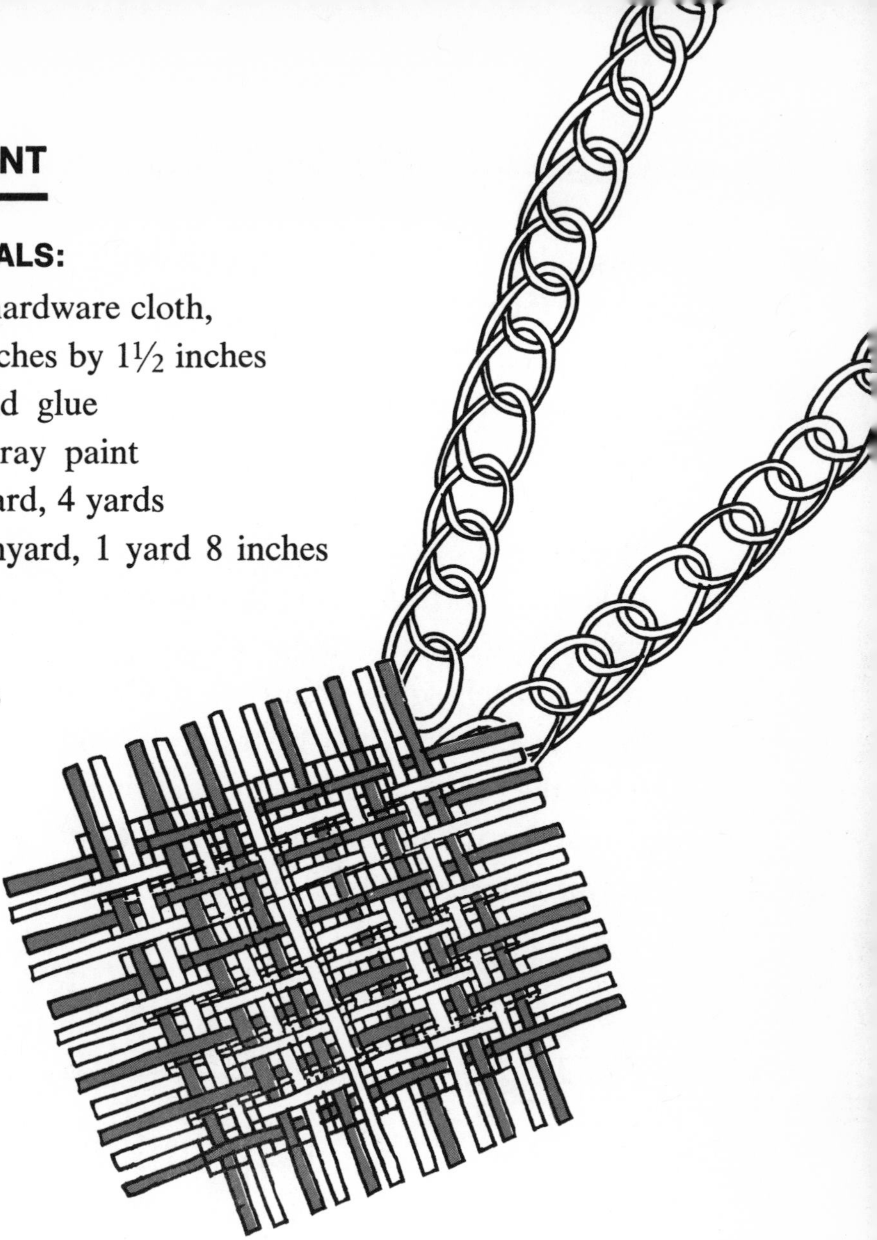

STEPS:

1. Trim the rough ends off the hardware cloth with tin snips. Apply glue to the rough places. Let the glue dry.
2. Spray both sides of the hardware cloth black. Let the paint dry.

3. Cut sixteen lengths of black lanyard, each 2¾ inches, and eight lengths of red lanyard, each 2¾ inches.

4. Beginning at the upper right corner, loosely weave a strand of red or black lanyard horizontally in and out of the upper half of the squares. Your pendant will be more interesting if you do not weave in and out of every square but sometimes skip over one or two squares. Let part of the lanyard extend out equally at each end of the row. Weave a red or black piece of lanyard horizontally in the bottom half of the same row (Figure 1). Continue weaving two rows of lanyard in each square until all the squares are filled. Alternate red and black strands as you wish.

5. Turn the pendant so that the weaving is vertical. Beginning at the upper right corner, weave a strand of lanyard horizontally in the upper half of the row.

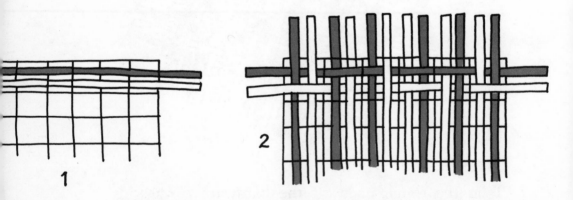

Weave in and out of the already filled squares, occasionally skipping over one or two squares (Figure 2). Let part of each strand extend out equally at each end of the row.

6. To make the chain, tie a knot 3 inches from the end of the remaining red lanyard, leaving a ¾-inch loop (Figure 3).

7. Hold the knot in your left hand with the loop hanging down and the lanyard behind it. With your right hand, insert the lanyard up through the loop and pull down to form another loop (Figure 4).

8. Insert the lanyard up through the second loop, and pull down to form another loop. Continue in the same way until 2½ inches of lanyard remain.

9. Insert the lanyard up through the last loop as before. Insert the end in the space between the last two loops, and pull tight (Figure 5).

10. Slip one end of the chain under a piece of lanyard at one corner of the pendant. Tie the ends of the chain together (Figure 6).

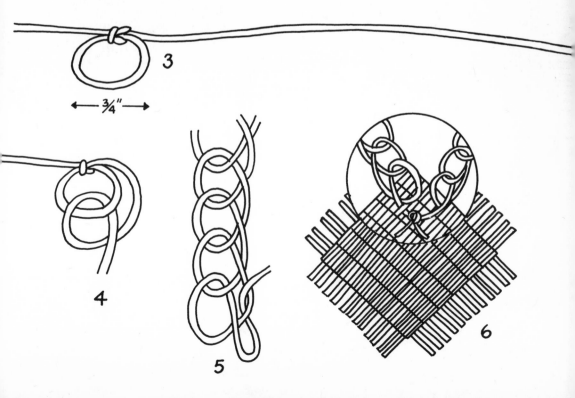

3

←— ¾" —→

4

5

6

WEAVING ON A CARDBOARD LOOM

POTHOLDER

MATERIALS:

6 men's heavy socks, of several colors
2 men's thin socks, of one color

TOOLS:

ruler
pencil
heavy cardboard, 7¼ inches by 9½ inches
scissors
paper clip

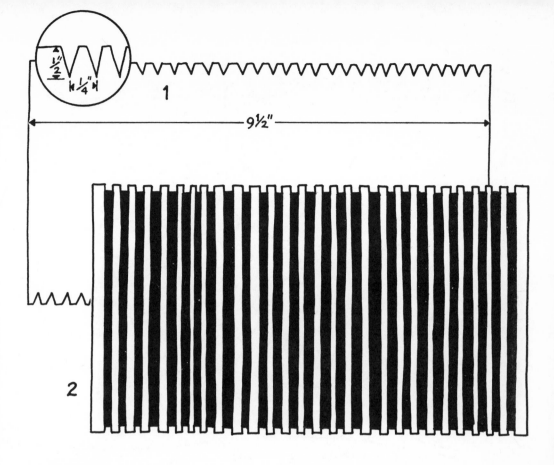

1

9½"

2

STEPS:

1. Along both long sides of the cardboard, cut twenty-seven notches ½ inch deep and ¼ inch apart. Begin at the center and work in both directions. This cardboard is the loom (Figure 1).

2. From the heavy socks, cut twenty-seven rings, each 1½ inches wide. Do not cut rings from the foot.

3. Slip one ring into the first notch at the top and bottom of the loom. The ring will go around the cardboard. Continue slipping each ring into the matching top and bottom notches. Arrange the colors as you wish. The rings are the warp (Figure 2).

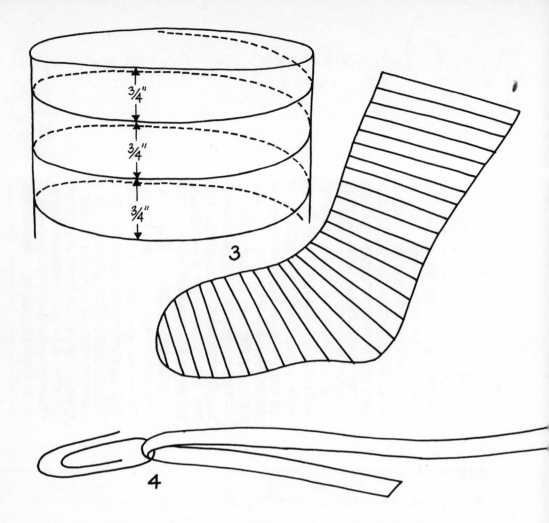

3

4

4. From each thin sock, cut one long strip about ¾ inch wide. Begin at the top of the sock and cut around and around down to the toe of the sock (Figure 3). Thread one end of the strip into the paper clip, which is the shuttle (Figure 4). Tie the other end of the strip to the outside warp ring at the upper right corner.

5. Weave horizontally under the second warp ring, over the third, and continue across in the same way.

6. For the second row, weave horizontally under the

first warp ring at the left, over the second, and continue across to the right side, keeping the second row ¼ inch below the first row (Figure 5).

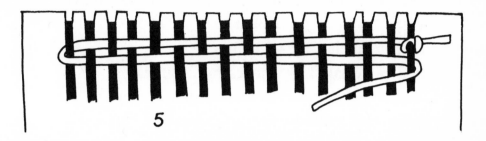

5

7. Weave the third row exactly as you did the first, and the fourth row exactly as you did the second. Continue weaving in this way, loosely enough to keep the edges straight. When the weaver becomes short, tie on another strip and continue weaving.
8. When you reach the bottom of the loom, turn it over and continue weaving until the second side is complete. Tie the weaver to a side warp ring and cut off.
9. Bend the cardboard loom in the center and slip the potholder off.
10. Thread a paper clip with a strip of thin sock, and sew one end of the potholder shut with an overcast stitch. Bring each stitch under the end warp rings (Figure 6). Knot the ends of the strip to a warp ring, and cut off.

6

CRAZY PILLOW

MATERIALS:

leather or leatherlike material, two or three colors,
   with a total measurement
   of 16½ inches by 46 inches
cotton material, 11½ inches by 22 inches
discarded nylon hose, 15 pairs, or cotton batting
   for pillow stuffing
household glue

TOOLS:

ruler
pencil
scissors
heavy cardboard,
   11½ inches by 16½ inches
masking tape
straight pins
needle and thread
   or sewing machine

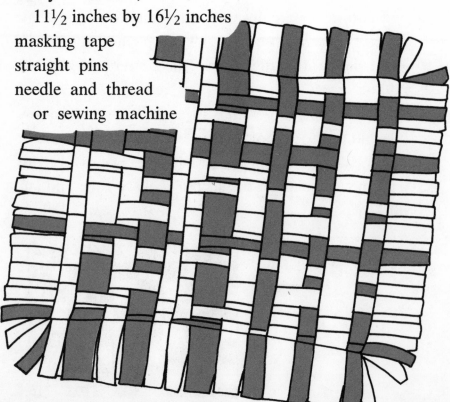

STEPS:

1. From the leather or leatherlike material, measure and cut seven strips, each 1 inch wide by 16½ inches long, and nine strips, each ½ inch wide by 16½ inches long. Cut some of the strips from each color. This is one group of strips. Cut three more groups of the same sizes.

2. Lay the cardboard on a flat surface with a shorter side toward you. Lay one group of strips side by side vertically on the cardboard. Mix the colors and widths as you wish. The strips should cover the cardboard. Tape each strip separately to the cardboard at both ends, letting the tape extend 1 inch onto the strips and 2 inches onto the back of the cardboard (Figure 1). These strips are the warp.

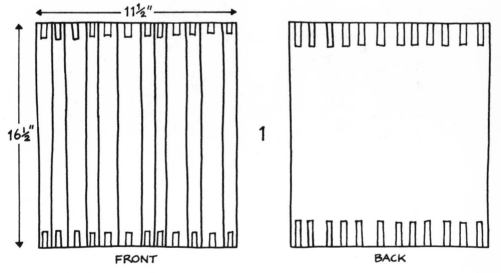

FRONT BACK

3. Use a second group of strips as weft. Beginning at the right side, 2½ inches from the top, weave one strip horizontally across to the left side, weaving over one

or two warp strips, then under one or two, and so on any way you wish. Let the ends extend equally on both sides. Do not try to keep the pattern the same (Figure 2).

4. Weave another strip, perhaps of a different color and width, just below the first strip over and under as you wish, but do not weave exactly the same way as you did the first strip (Figure 2).

5. Weave the third strip in the same manner, but as you weave check each warp strip. Has one of the weft strips gone *over* each warp strip at least once? If it hasn't, go over that strip this time. Has one of the weft strips gone *under* each warp strip at least once? If it hasn't, go under this time (Figure 2).

6. Continue weaving strip after strip, checking at every third strip as you did before. Stop weaving 2½ inches from the bottom of the warp.

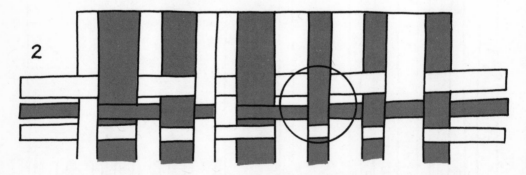

2

7. Remove the tape and cardboard. Lift the top of each strip, and with a toothpick apply a small drop of glue between it and the strip underneath it. Let the glue dry. Turn the pillow covering over carefully. Glue

all of the strips now at the top as you did the first ones. The ends of the strips, extending loosely on all four sides, will make the fringe.

8. Make another pillow covering the same way.

9. Lay the two pillow coverings together, right side out. Pin together in each corner. With a needle and thread (or sewing machine), using a running stitch, sew the pillow coverings together on three sides, $\frac{3}{8}$ of an inch inside the fringe (Figure 3). Remove the pins.

10. Double the cotton material, wrong side out. With a needle and thread (or sewing machine), using a running stitch, sew the three open sides $\frac{1}{2}$ inch from the edge, leaving a 5-inch opening on one side (Figure 4).

11. Turn inside out, and stuff with nylon hose or cotton batting. Sew the opening shut, using a running stitch.

12. Put the stuffed pillow inside the woven covering. Sew the opening shut, using a running stitch.

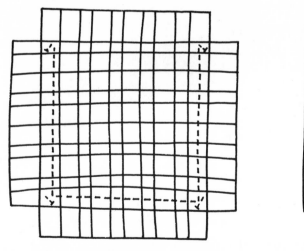

3

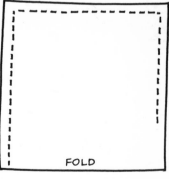

FOLD

4

COVERED COAT HANGER

MATERIALS:

red rug yarn, 17 yards 1 foot
black rug yarn, 6 yards
wooden hanger, 1 inch by 17 inches by ⅜ inch thick
   (excluding wire part)

TOOLS:

2 pieces heavy cardboard,
   each 2 inches by 10 inches
heavy cord, 80 inches
scissors
ruler
pencil
paper clip
straight pins
upholstery needle

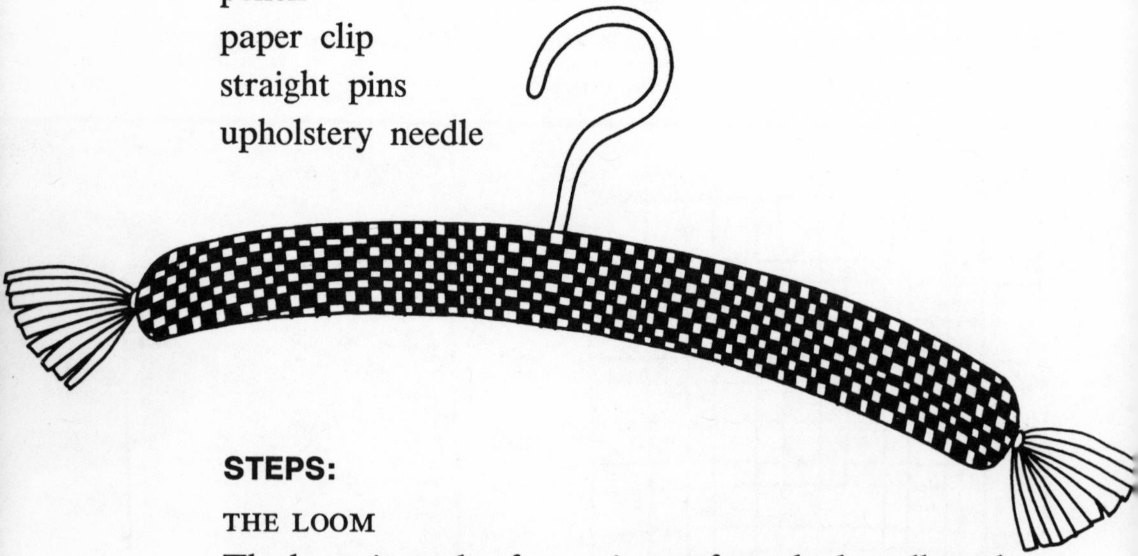

STEPS:

THE LOOM

The loom is made of two pieces of notched cardboard
placed 10 inches apart. It will be held together by the
warp strands of yarn threaded into the cardboard

notches. As you weave horizontally, the space between the cardboards will be filled. Then the bottom
cardboard will be moved farther down the warp
strands to allow room for more weaving.

1. *Making the loom.* Along a long side of each piece of
cardboard, make twenty-one notches ½ inch deep
and ¼ inch apart. Begin at the center and work in
both directions. Three quarters of an inch in from
each upper corner, pierce a small hole. Cut a 40-inch
length of cord. Thread the cord through the holes of
one cardboard and tie the cord together (Figure 1).
Cut two 20-inch lengths of cord. Put one length of
cord through each hole of the other cardboard, and
tie a knot large enough to keep the cord from slipping
through. This is the loom (Figure 2). Loop the long

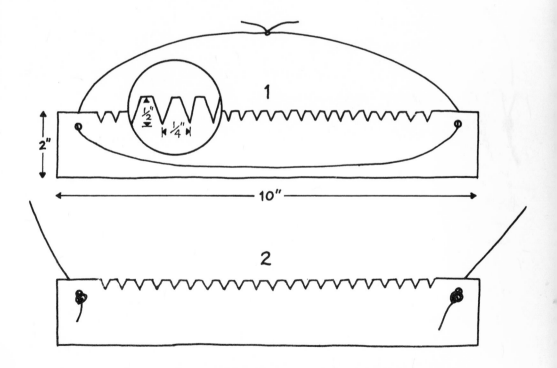

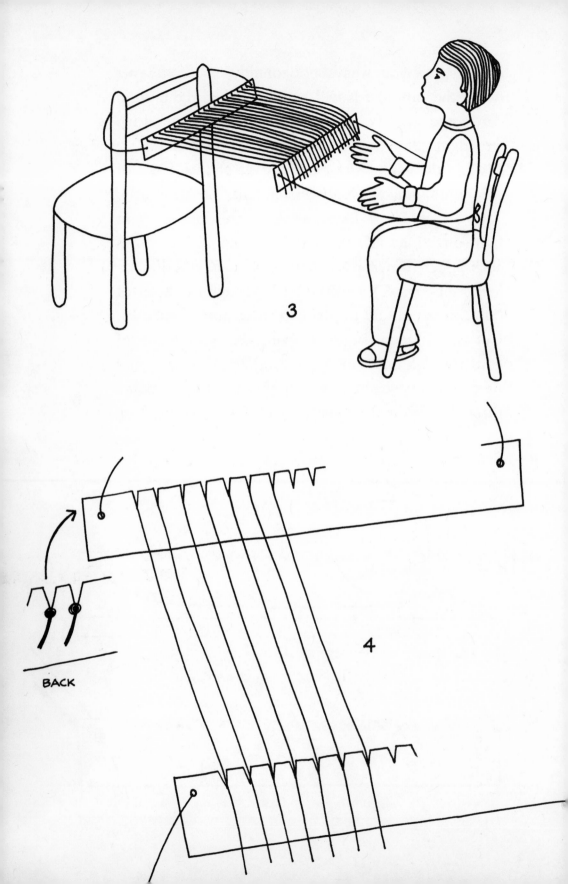

3

4

BACK

cord of the first cardboard over the back of a kitchen chair. After threading the loom, you will tie the two cords of the second cardboard around your waist. The cardboard will be in front of you, and the long ends of yarn will hang down between the cardboard and your body (Figure 3).

2. *Threading the loom.* Cut twenty-one strands of red yarn, each 26 inches long. Tie a loose knot 3½ inches from both ends of each strand. Slip a strand of yarn into each notch of the first cardboard with a knot resting on the back of the notch. Ten inches from the cardboard, slip the first strand of yarn into the first notch of the second cardboard. Slip the second strand into the second notch, and so on across in the same way. These strands are the warp (Figure 4).

3. The paper clip is your shuttle. Thread it with a strand of black yarn 24 inches long (Figure 5). At the upper right corner of the warp, tie the end of the yarn to the first strand of warp.

5

4. Weave horizontally under the second strand of warp, over the third, and continue all the way across.

5. To start the second row, which runs from left to right, continue with the same yarn. Weave it under the first strand, over the second strand, under the third, and on across. Weave close to the first row (Figure 6).

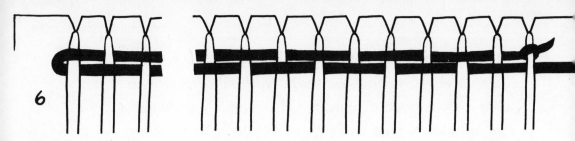

Push the stitches up toward the first row with the shuttle if necessary.

6. Weave the third row as in step 4. Weave the fourth row as in step 5. Continue weaving, first step 4 and then step 5, keeping each row close to the last. When you have woven about 8 inches, untie the cord from your waist. Move the cardboard down the warp so that it rests against the knots 3½ inches from the ends. Tie the cord around your waist again. Move the chair holding the loom away from you when necessary to keep the warp fairly tight. When your yarn becomes short, tie another strand on and continue weaving.

7. When the weaving reaches the knots (3½ inches from the end of the warp), tie the black yarn to a strand of warp on one side of the loom. Cut off. Untie the cord from your waist, and carefully lift the loom off the chair.

8. Fold the weaving lengthwise, and at the exact center draw it carefully over the wire part of the hanger and let it rest on the wooden part. Be certain that any knots in the weft are on the underside.

9. With straight pins, pin the weaving together at the bottom of the hanger, beginning at the center and pinning toward the ends.

10. Thread an upholstery needle with 36 inches of red yarn. Beginning at one end, loop the yarn twice around the red warp threads and tie securely. Sew the weaving together all the way across the bottom of the hanger with an overcast stitch (Figure 7). When you reach the end, loop the yarn twice around the red warp threads, and tie securely. Cut off.

11. Cut off the warp threads 1¼ inches from both ends of the hanger.

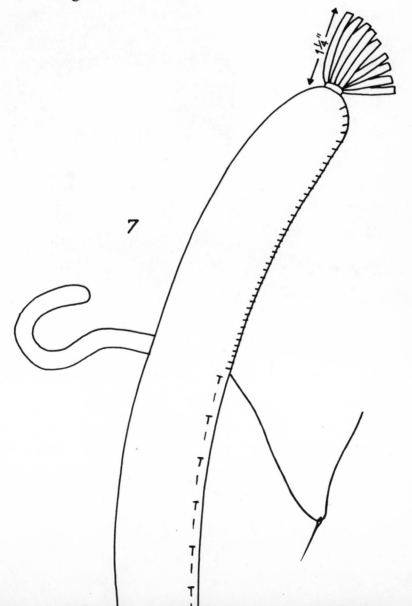

7

SCARF

MATERIALS:

4-ply variegated yarn, 104 yards

TOOLS:

2 pieces heavy cardboard, each 2 inches by 10 inches
heavy cord, 80 inches
ruler
pencil
scissors
paper clip

STEPS:

THE LOOM

The loom is made of two pieces of notched cardboard placed 10 inches apart. It will be held together by warp strands of yarn threaded into the cardboard notches. As you weave horizontally, the space between the cardboards will be filled. Then the bottom cardboard will be moved farther down the warp strands to allow room for more weaving.

1. *Making the loom.* Along a long side of each piece of cardboard, make 27 notches ½ inch deep and ¼ inch apart. Begin at the center and work in both directions. Three quarters of an inch in from each upper corner, pierce a small hole. Cut a 40-inch length of cord. Thread the cord through each hole of one cardboard, and tie the cord together (Figure 1). Cut two 20-inch

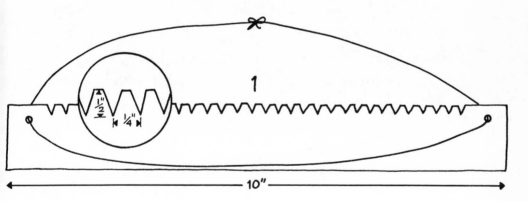

lengths of cord. Put one length of cord through each hole of the other cardboard, and tie a knot large enough to keep the cord from slipping through. This is the loom (Figure 2). Loop the long cord of the first card-

2

2"

10"

board over the back of a kitchen chair. After threading the loom, you will tie the two cords of the second cardboard around your waist. The cardboard will be in front of you, and the long ends of yarn will hang down between the cardboard and your body (Figure 3).

2. *Threading the loom.* Cut fifty-four strands of yarn, each 42 inches long. Tie two strands together loosely, 6 inches from one end. Slip the double strand of yarn into the first notch of the first cardboard with the knot resting on the back of the notch. Ten inches from the cardboard, slip the double strand of yarn into the first notch of the second cardboard. Slip the second double strand into the second notch, and so on across in the same way. These strands are the warp (Figure 4).

3. The paper clip is your shuttle. Thread it with a strand of yarn 48 inches long (Figure 5). Pull the ends even.

5

At the upper right corner of the warp, tie the ends of the yarn to the first double strand of warp.

4. Weave horizontally under the next two double strands of warp, over the next double strand, under the next

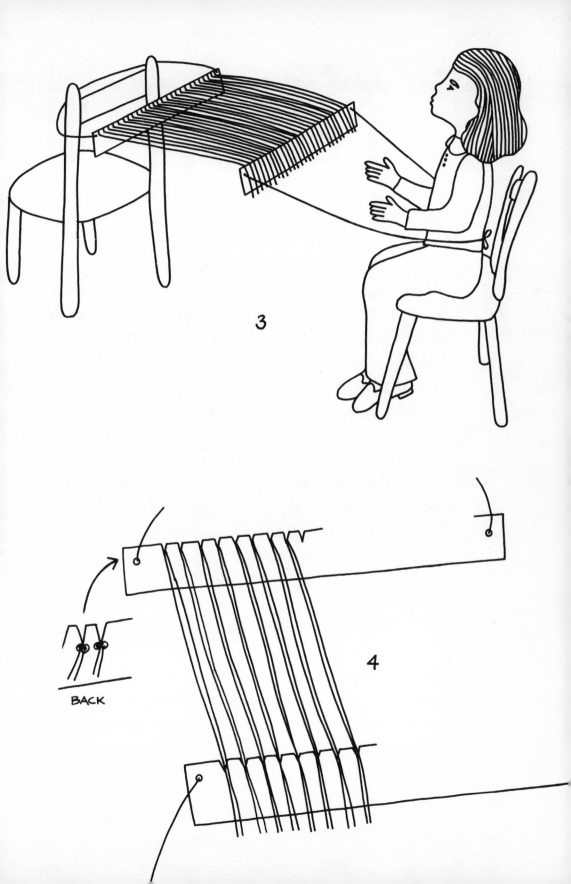

3

BACK

4

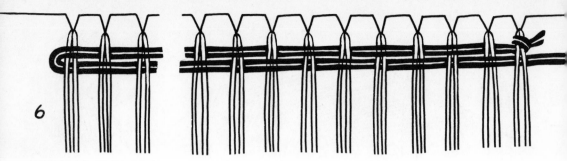

two double strands, and continue all the way across. You will be weaving over the last two double strands.

5. To start the second horizontal row, which runs from left to right, continue with the same yarn. Weave it under the first two double strands, over the next double strand, under the next two double strands, over the next double strand, and on across. Weave close to the first row (Figure 6). Push the weaving up toward the first row with the shuttle if necessary.

6. Weave the third row as in step 4. Weave the fourth row as in step 5. Continue weaving, repeating first step 4 and then step 5. Keep each row close to the last until the weaving is within 2 inches of the cardboard. Untie the cord from your waist, move the cardboard 11 inches farther down the warp, and tie the cord around your waist again. Move the chair holding the loom away from you when necessary to keep the warp fairly tight. When your yarn becomes short, tie another double strand to it and continue weaving. When the weaving is within 2 inches of the cardboard, untie the cord from your waist, move the cardboard 11 inches farther down the warp, and tie the cord around your waist again.

7. When you have woven 6 inches from the end of the warp, tie the weaver to a strand of warp on either side of the loom. Cut off, and lift the loom off the chair. If you wish, untie the knots that held the warp on the loom.

8. Beginning at the lower left side, tie each double strand loosely to the next double strand. The last double strand will not be looped. A half inch below the loops, tie a knot in the first double strand. Then tie together the next two double strands. Continue across, tying each two double strands together. A half inch below the knots, tie the first two double strands together. Continue tying each two double strands together all the way across (Figure 7). The last double strand will be left over; ½ inch down, tie a knot in it. The additional lengths of yarn are the fringe. Finish the other end of the scarf in the same way.

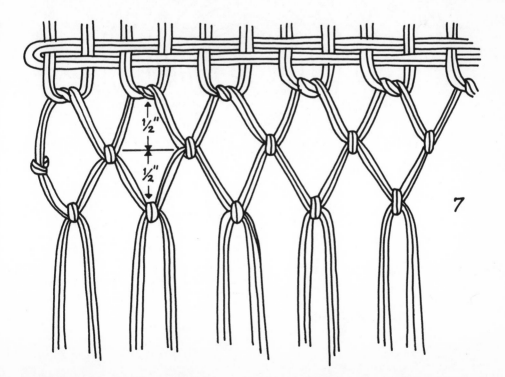

7

BASKET WEAVING

TABLE MAT

MATERIALS:
#4 (thick) reed, 5¾ yards
#2 (thin) reed, 18 yards

TOOLS:
heavy scissors
ruler
bucket of water

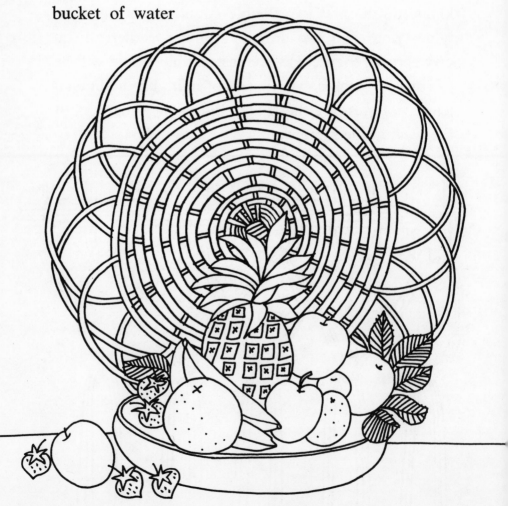

STEPS:

1. Cut eight spokes of #4 reed, each 24 inches long, and a spoke 14 inches long.
2. Soak the spokes and the thin reed (for weavers) in water for at least half an hour to make them flexible. (As you weave, dip the table mat and the reed in water occasionally to keep them moist.)
3. Place four 24-inch spokes closely together and parallel to each other. Place the other 24-inch spokes over the first four at right angles, so they form a cross. Lay the 14-inch spoke in the center of one group of spokes, with one end even with the ends of the other four (Figure 1).

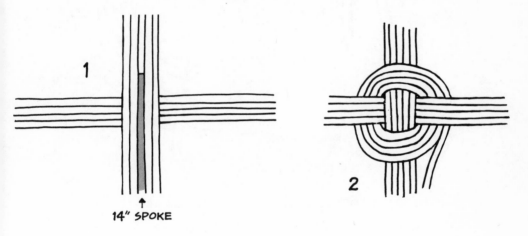

14" SPOKE

4. Cut a 6-yard weaver from the #2 reed. Holding one end of the weaver, bind the spokes together (hold them in place with your left hand) by weaving in a clockwise direction. Weave the reed tightly over one top set of spokes, under the second set, over the third set, and under the fourth. Weave around the spokes in the same way three more times (Figure 2).

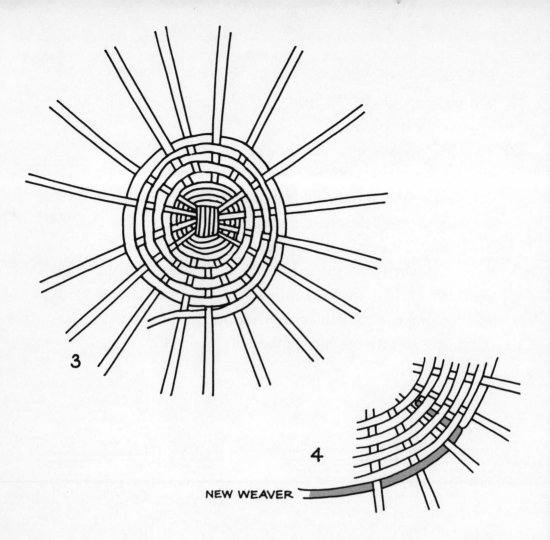

3

4

NEW WEAVER

5. Separate the spokes so they are arranged like the spokes of a wheel. In a clockwise direction, weave over the first spoke, under the second, over the third. Continue weaving around and around, keeping each row close to the last (Figure 3). When the weaver is very short, bend it down sharply and insert the end into the part already woven. Cut another 6-yard length of weaver. Insert the first inch into the mat, and continue weaving (Figure 4).

6. When 9 inches of the spokes remain, cut the weaver off and bend sharply about an inch into the mat.

7. Bend one spoke clockwise behind the first spoke next to it, in front of the second spoke, and insert one inch into the mat just before you reach the third spoke (Figure 5). Continue all around the mat, bending each spoke the same way.

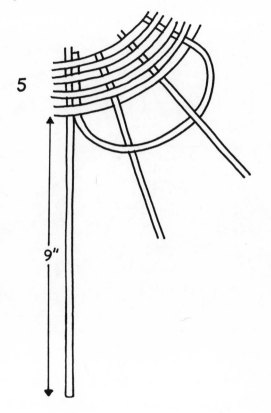

TINY GRASS BASKET

MATERIALS:
field grass
spray lacquer or clear spray varnish

TOOLS:
scissors
ruler

STEPS:

1. Gather long, green stems or blades of field grass. For spokes, cut eight sturdy stems, each 11 inches long. For weavers, use stems or blades a little smaller in diameter.

2. Place four spokes closely together and parallel to each other. Place the other spokes over the first four at right angles, so they form a cross (Figure 1). Holding one end of a weaver, bind the spokes together (hold

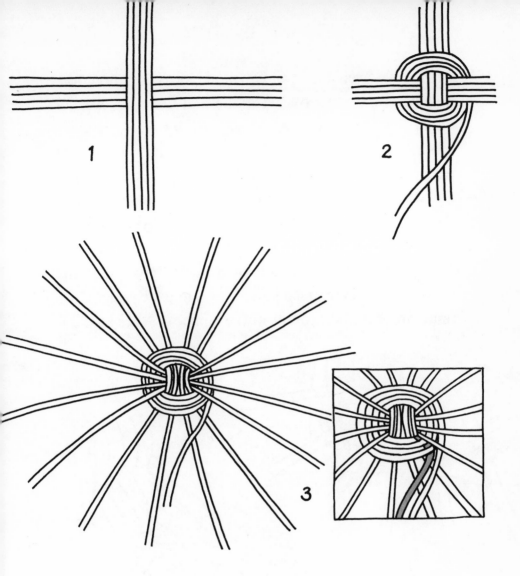

them in place with your left hand) by weaving in a clockwise direction. Weave tightly over the one top set of spokes, under the next set, over the third set, and under the fourth. Weave around the spokes in the same way three more times (Figure 2).

3. Separate the spokes so they are arranged like the spokes of a wheel. Add another weaver by inserting ½ inch of one end into the woven part (Figure 3).

4. Using two weavers, weave in a clockwise direction, placing one weaver over a spoke and the other weaver under the same spoke. Cross the weavers between spokes. This is called "pairing." Place the weaver that went over the first spoke under the second spoke and the weaver that went under the first spoke over the second spoke (Figure 4). When a weaver becomes short, bend sharply and insert the last ½ inch into the woven part. Insert ½ inch of a new weaver into the woven part, bend sharply, and continue weaving. Continue around and around in the same way (Figure 5).

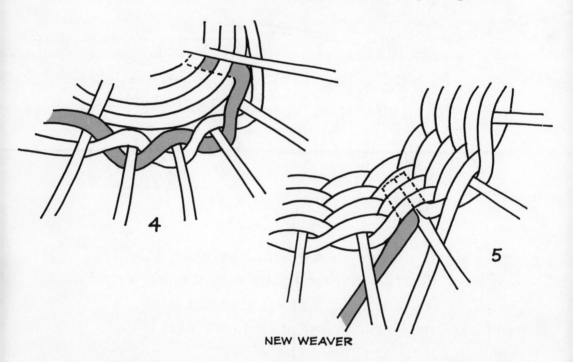

NEW WEAVER

5. When the weaving is 2½ inches in diameter, bend each spoke up. Continue weaving, holding the spokes up as you weave, to form the sides of the basket (Figure

6). When the sides are woven 1¼ inches high, bend both weavers sharply, insert down into the weaving, and cut off.

6. Bend one spoke clockwise behind the first spoke next to it, then in front of the second spoke, and insert ¼ inch down into the side of the basket just before you reach the third spoke (Figure 7). Continue all the way around the basket.

7. Spray the inside and outside of the basket with lacquer or varnish several times, allowing each coat to dry between sprayings.

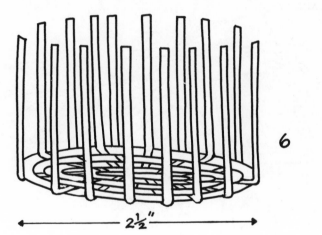

6

2½"

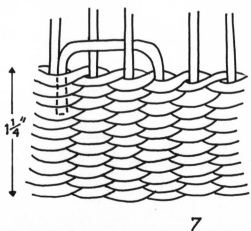

1¼"

7

BIRDHOUSE

MATERIALS:

#4 (thick) reed, 6½ yards
#2 (thin) reed, 32 yards
heavy cord, 30 inches

TOOLS:

heavy scissors
ruler
bucket of water

STEPS:

1. Cut eight spokes of #4 reed, each 16 inches long, and a spoke 9 inches long. Soak the spokes and the thin reed in water for at least half an hour to make them flexible. (As you weave, dip the reeds in water occasionally to keep them moist.)

2. Place four 16-inch spokes closely together and parallel to each other. Place the other 16-inch spokes over the first four at right angles, so they form a cross. Lay the 9-inch spoke in the center of one group of 16-inch spokes with one end even with the ends of the other four (Figure 1).

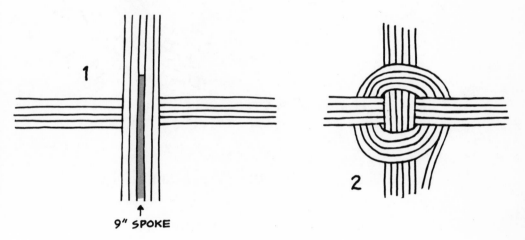

9" SPOKE

3. Cut a 6-yard weaver from the #2 reed. Holding one end of the weaver, bind the spokes together (hold them in place with your left hand) by weaving in a clockwise direction. Weave the reed tightly over one top set of spokes, under the second set, over the third set, and under the fourth. Weave around the spokes in the same way three more times (Figure 2).

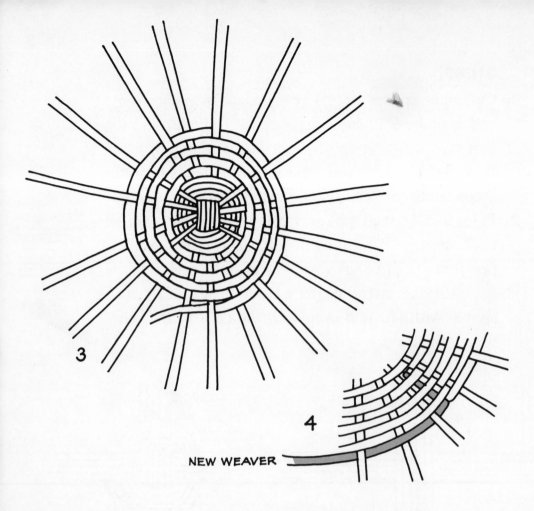

3

4

NEW WEAVER

4. Separate the spokes so they are arranged like the spokes of a wheel. In a clockwise direction, weave over the first spoke, under the second, and over the third. Continue weaving around and around, keeping each row close to the last (Figure 3). When the weaver is very short, bend it down sharply and insert the end into the part already woven. Cut another 6-yard length of weaver. Insert the first ½ inch into the woven part (Figure 4). Continue weaving around and around. This is the roof the birdhouse.

5. When the woven part is 4 inches in diameter, bend each spoke down. Continue weaving in the same way, holding the spokes down as you weave to make the sides of the birdhouse (Figure 5).

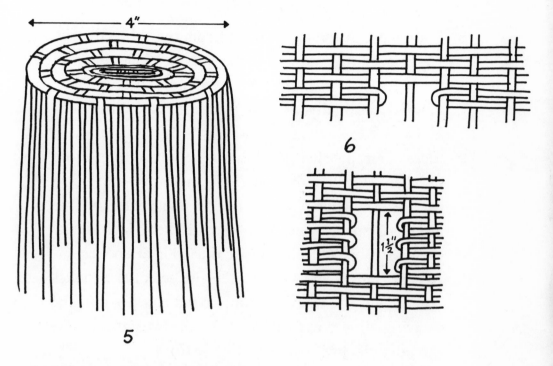

5

6

6. When the sides are 2 inches deep, reverse the weaver around one spoke and begin weaving in a counter-clockwise direction to leave an opening for the door. When you reach the next to last spoke on this row, reverse the weaver around the spoke and again weave in a clockwise direction. This will leave one spoke extending across the doorway. Continue weaving, re-versing the weaving at the end of each row until the doorway is 1½ inches high (Figure 6).

7. Again begin weaving clockwise around and around

the birdhouse, over and under all of the spokes. Continue until the birdhouse is 5¼ inches high. Cut the weaver off and bend sharply about an inch into the weaving. Cut away the reed that extends across the doorway. Set the birdhouse aside.

8. For the porch, cut eight spokes from the #4 reed, each 10 inches long, and one spoke 6 inches long. Soak in water for at least half an hour to make them flexible. (Dip occasionally as you weave to keep the reed moist.)

9. Place four parallel 10-inch spokes over four more parallel 10-inch spokes at right angles, so they form a cross. Lay the 6-inch spoke in the center of one group of spokes with one end of the 6-inch spoke even with one set of ends of the 10-inch spokes.

10. Repeat steps 3 and 4. When 2½ inches of the spokes remain, cut the weaver off and bend sharply into the weaving. Insert each spoke into the weaving beside the next clockwise spoke (Figure 7).

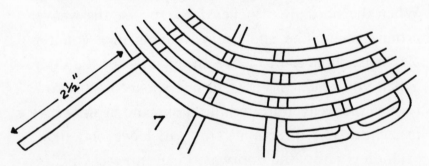

11. Be certain both the birdhouse and porch are moist and flexible. Set the birdhouse on the center of the porch. Insert each spoke of the birdhouse through

the weaving of the porch. Weave each spoke into the porch, and bring it out on the top side. Cut off spokes (Figure 8).

12. Insert each end of the cord through a few weavers at the top on opposite sides of the birdhouse, and tie the ends together across the roof (Figure 9). Loop the cord over the branch of a tree or bush.

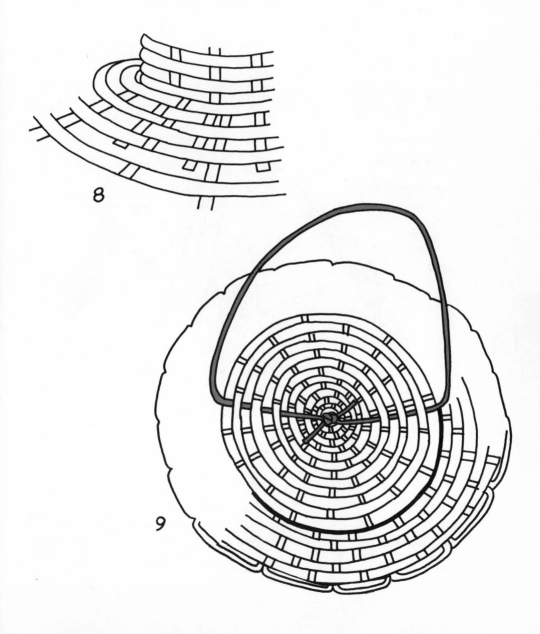

8

9

EASTER BASKET

MATERIALS:

#4 (thick) reed, 12¼ yards
#2 (thin) reed, 49 yards
pink fabric dye
green fabric dye

TOOLS:

yardstick or ruler
heavy scissors
2 kettles
bucket of water
table fork
rubber bands

STEPS:

1. Mix the green fabric dye in one kettle and pink fabric dye in another, according to directions on the package for kettle dyeing, but use twice as much dye as recommended.

2. You will dye green 35 yards of #2 reed and 10 yards of #4 reed. Cut and wind the reed into a circle small enough to fit into one kettle, and fasten with a rubber band. Put into the green dye. Lift out with a fork every two minutes to check the shade. When it is one shade darker than you wish, remove reed from the dye. Put in cold water for a few minutes to remove the excess dye.

3. You will dye pink 12 yards of #2 reed and 2¼ yards of #4 reed. Repeat step 2, using the pink dye.

4. From the #4 green reed, cut ten spokes, each 18 inches long and one spoke 10 inches long. Keep the spokes moist as you work by dipping in water occasionally.

5. Place five 18-inch spokes closely together and parallel to each other. Place the other 18-inch spokes over the first five at right angles, so they form a cross. Lay the 10-inch spoke in the center of either set of spokes, with one end of the spoke even with the ends of the other five (Figure 1).

6. Cut a green weaver about 6 yards long from the #2 reed. (Keep the weaver moist as you work by dipping in water occasionally.) Holding one end of the weaver, bind the spokes together by weaving in a clockwise

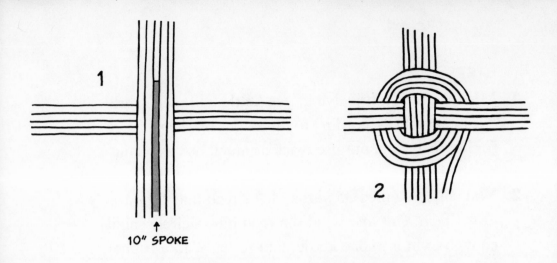

1

↑
10" SPOKE

2

direction. Weave the reed tightly over one top set of spokes, under the next set, over the third, and under the fourth. Weave around the spokes in the same way three more times (Figure 2).

7. Separate the spokes so they are arranged like the spokes of a wheel. Weave in a clockwise direction over the first spoke, under the second, over the third, and continue weaving around and around (Figure 3).

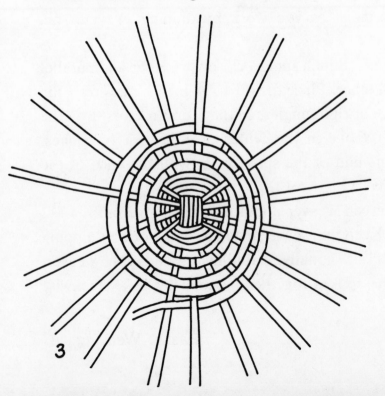

3

When the weaver becomes very short, bend it sharply down and insert the end into the woven part. Cut another green weaver. Insert the first inch down into the woven part, and continue weaving (Figure 4).

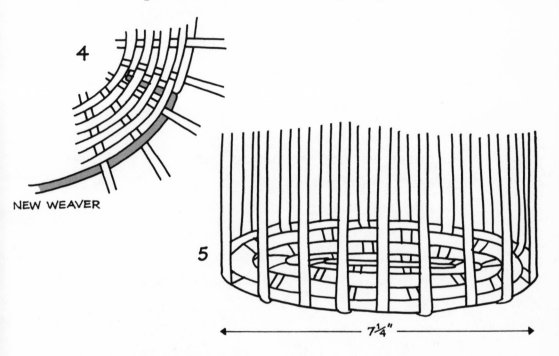

NEW WEAVER

4

5

7¼"

8. When the diameter of the basket bottom is 7¼ inches, bend each spoke up (Figure 5). Add one more green weaver by inserting an inch into the woven part. Keep the spokes up as you weave. Using the two weavers, let one go over a spoke and the other go under the same spoke. Cross the weavers between spokes. This is called "pairing." Let the weaver that went over the first spoke go under the second spoke and the weaver that went under the first spoke go over the second spoke (Figure 6). Continue weaving around the bas-

6

ket five times, keeping the rows close together. Cut off one weaver an inch from the basket. Insert the end into the woven part.

9. Cut two pink weavers. You will use them together as one weaver. Insert them an inch into the woven part. Use the remaining green weaver as the second weaver. Continue weaving around the basket as you did before, letting the green weaver go over a spoke and the double pink weaver go under the same spoke. Cross the weavers, and let the green weaver go under the next spoke and the double pink weaver go over the same spoke (Figure 7). Continue weaving for seven rows.

7

10. Cut off the pink weaver an inch from the basket, and insert into the woven part. Add a green weaver, to take the place of the pink weaver, and continue weaving in the same way for four rows.

11. Add two more green weavers. You will use them together as one weaver. Insert them an inch into the woven part. Continue to weave one double weaver over a spoke and another double weaver under the same spoke. Cross the weavers *twice* between each spoke (Figure 8). This is called "double pairing," and it will make the rim of the basket very firm. Continue weaving around the basket for two rows. Cut off the weavers an inch from the basket, and insert all the ends into the woven part.

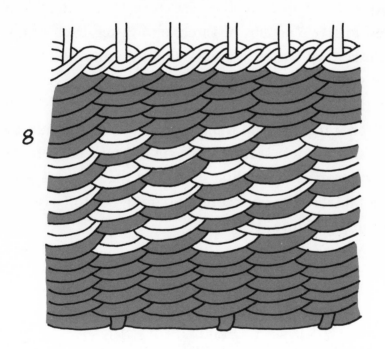

8

12. If the ends of spokes seem dry, soak in water for a few minutes. Bend each spoke clockwise toward the next spoke. Insert through the top row of weaving to the inside of the basket. Cut off the ends (Figure 9).

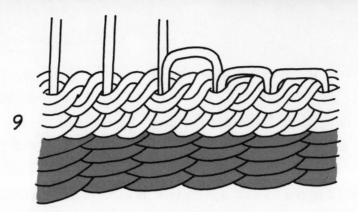

9

13. To make the handle, cut six lengths of #4 green reed, each 27 inches, and three lengths of #4 pink reed, each 27 inches. Fasten the pink reeds togther with a rubber band an inch from the ends. Divide the green reed into two groups of three, and fasten each group together with rubber bands at both ends. If reed is dry soak for half an hour.

14. Bind all three groups together at one end firmly with a rubber band. Braid the three sets of reed tightly by crossing the left set over the middle set (the left set now becomes the middle set), then the right set over the middle set, and continue until all the reed is braided (Figure 10).

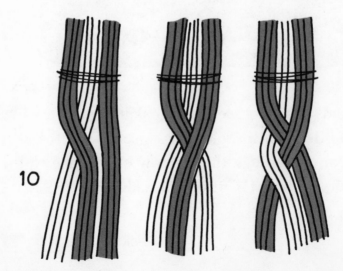

10

15. Spread the last inch of the end of the braid apart. Cut off the rubber bands. Insert each reed of one end into the weaving near the bottom of the basket on the inside (Figure 11). Do the same with the other end on the opposite side.

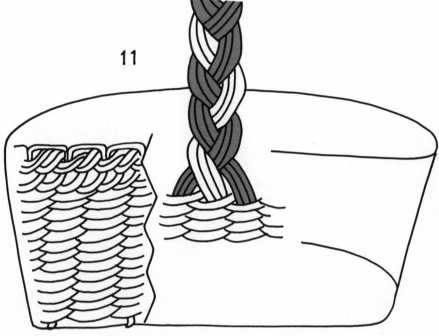

11

16. Cut a 37-inch length of #2 green reed. Bind the center of the reed around the handle twice at the top of the basket on both sides. Cross the ends of the reed on the outside of the basket, and insert them to the inside of the basket an inch from the top. Make the cross about ¼ inch wider than the basket handle. Cross again on the inside of the basket, and insert to the outside 2 inches from the top. Cross again on the outside, and insert to the inside at the bottom of the

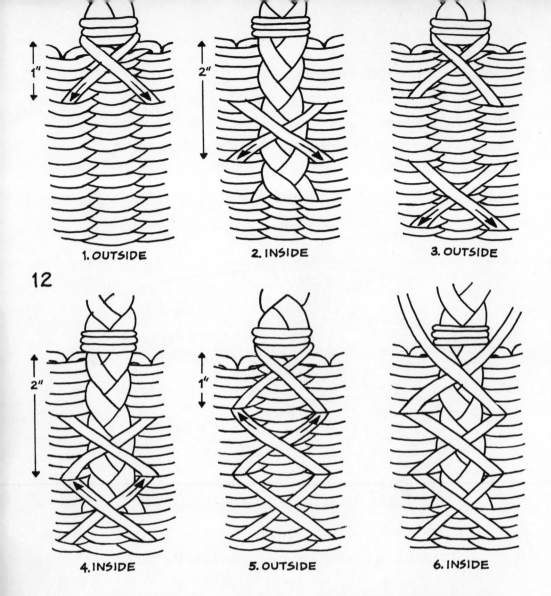

1. OUTSIDE

2. INSIDE

3. OUTSIDE

12

4. INSIDE

5. OUTSIDE

6. INSIDE

basket. On the inside cross again, and bring to the outside about two inches from the top. Make another cross, and insert to the inside about one inch from the top. Cross again and bring the reed to the top of the basket (Figure 12). Bind it around the handle once, and insert sharply down under the binding on the inside. Cut off.

94   Basket Weaving

CONCLUSION

When you finish weaving these items, try other colors, sizes, and designs. Look around to find different kinds of flexible scrap materials. Experiment to find new things to weave and different ways to weave. The variations you develop will make your projects more individual and original.

ABOUT THE AUTHOR

Born in Montpelier, Idaho, Alice Thompson Gilbreath attended the College of Idaho in Caldwell. Later she continued her studies at the University of Tulsa, in Oklahoma, and at Trinity University, in San Antonio, Texas. She has taught school and worked with youth groups, including Cub Scouts, Girl Scouts, day camps, and Sunday school. The author of several children's books, Mrs. Gilbreath lives in Bartlesville, Oklahoma.

ABOUT THE ARTIST

A native of Watertown, New York, Judith Hoffman Corwin is a graduate of Pratt Institute, in Brooklyn, with the degree of B.F.A. For some years she has been a free-lance illustrator and designer, and in 1974 her work was included in the annual exhibition of the Society of Illustrators. She, her husband, and their small son now live in New York City.